BEAUTIFUL COLOURS

Reflections on the Problem of Racism

I0102221

Osman Alimamy Sankoh
(Mallam O.)

Sierra Leonean Writers Series

Beautiful Colours

Reflections on the Problem of Racism

Copyright © Osman Alimamy Sankoh (Mallam O.) 2016

ISBN 978-99910-54-48-3

First published 1999 by
Sierra Leone e.V.
Vogelpothsweg 24
D-44149 Dortmund, Germany

Dedicated to:

All of YOU
Who continue to strive in many ways
To ensure that
WE all live in a harmonious world
Irrespective of OUR
Race, colour, religion, ethnic group, nationality,
gender, disability, economic status,
sexual orientation ...

Foreword

It is difficult to find someone openly agreeing that he or she discriminates against another based on skin colour, race, social status, life-style, and so on. But we certainly do discriminate against others in various forms and for various reasons. Human relationships are complex and as such there are many possibilities for some sort of discrimination to occur. It is this complexity of the 'issue' that Mallam O. has embraced in this book with the objective of highlighting the fundamental propelling forces that cause us - blacks and whites - to discriminate against others. The reader will appreciate the author's easygoing and conversational style, one which makes it possible to understand the issues discussed. It will be difficult for anyone who has read this book not to recommend it further. I count on the support of the members in our union in Dortmund as well as those in all unions of Sierra Leoneans in Germany and elsewhere to assist in the distribution of this book.

Morie J. P. Bunduka, President, S.L.e.V.

Acknowledgements

This place has been reserved to express my gratitude to the many good people who freely discussed *racism* with me, especially LEONENET subscribers, and to my many friends and colleagues including Osman Sanneh, Morie Manyeh, Yusuf Bangura, Siaka Kroma, Richard Konteh, Crispin Webber, James Andrew Weima, Klaus Ludes, Ibrahim Abdullah, Suffyan Kargbo, Thomas Fischer, Carola Deppe, Usula Vogel, Linda Musa, Dietmar Doering, Magdalena Thöne, Fiona Cooke, Gitta Neumann, Pamela Mogoi Nyauntu, Helen Mueni K. Magolo, and Sheikh Umarr Kamara who read drafts of the book and made critical comments. Without such views and comments on this complex topic, a book like this would not have been worth writing. I would like to thank my wife, Jariatu and my children, Fatima, Fatmata and Christiana for their invaluable contribution in diverse ways to this product. I thank them especially for always allowing me to dedicate my books to other people.

Hello!

In this book, I shall be talking to you about different types of discrimination, stressing the fact that the most pervasive is discrimination based on skin colour. This is mainly a product of the interrelations between people described as 'black' and people described as 'white'. I have come to realise that a black person born and bred in Africa is as unconscious of his skin colour as a white person born and bred in the West; that is, until the two have cause to interact.

In order for everyone to live in harmony, we must overcome the tendency to discriminate against others based on their skin colour. I am therefore, not writing for any specific racial group and hope the book will appeal to you, no matter which racial group you belong to. Where I give local examples, I shall try to strengthen them by complementary pieces from elsewhere.

I shall talk about history, language, culture, politics, economics and religion, for they are the most common sources of unfair judgements and generalisations about others. My objective is to highlight the roles they have played in promoting discrimination based on skin colour

In some sections of the book, you will observe that I seem to be talking to myself. When you do so, please stop me, will you? Or can you? But certainly, I shall continue to have you in mind throughout, and even engage your participation at strategic points, by asking you to do certain things or answer certain questions.

My approach in this book will mainly be informal and conversational. The language will be as simple and straightforward as I can make it. From time to time, though, I may decide to change my style and become more rigorous and analytical. So when it becomes too hard or too easy, just sigh; that passage will not last very long. Similarly, I will be direct on some issues, and indirect on others. I shall however, try to present a balanced approach.

I hope that the discussion helps us ask ourselves intelligent questions about how we could each contribute to making ours a much more harmonious world, and maybe, come up with answers that we could live with.

What is discrimination?

A friend exclaimed: "I don't like it; this is discrimination!"

Have you ever heard someone say that? If you have, did you understand what the speaker was complaining about? If you did understand, did you agree with the speaker at the time?

If your answer to all the above questions is "yes," then you will find it easy to follow this discussion. If, however, you have heard the statement before but you did not understand what the person meant, then I implore you to read on with attention.

If you did not agree with the person, it meant that you thought the person was wrong in his or her conclusion. Let us see what opinion you will build up as you read.

What is *discrimination*?

To 'discriminate' can mean to see and note the difference, but without judgement. Look at this page. What is the difference between the colour of the words and the paper on which they are written? I have asked you to 'differentiate,' have I not?

Consider a hill and a plain. If I ask you to 'note the distinguishing features' between them, I am also asking you to 'discriminate;' but I am not asking you to make a judgement as to which of them is better.

Consider my friend's complaint again. He probably uttered those words after someone compared him unfavourably with others. When such a distinction is made, it may be evidence of *unfair discrimination* or of *discrimination against.* By the time you finish reading this book, you should be able to understand that when you discriminate against someone or something, you are exercising a preference for one at the expense of the other. I am sure that many real-life examples of unfair discrimination might have sprung to mind, so I shall mention just a few.

Many societies had unfairly discriminated against women. Even in Europe, women in

Switzerland started taking part in elections only in 1971. In some communities, religion and customs have been used or are still used to impose inferior roles on women. For instance, in mosques, women are not only separated from men, their place is at the back. Saudi women are not allowed to drive cars or deal directly with men. Under the Taliban, Afghan women were not allowed to speak in public or to work outside the home. It is difficult to find a woman heading a mosque. Similarly, the Roman Catholic and some Anglican Churches have been struggling with the question of ordaining female priests. In some Arab countries, women must veil their heads and faces in public. On the other hand, in the Western world, women are used as sex symbols in films and commercials just to please men.

However, it is important to note that a few countries in the developed and developing world, including some in the Muslim world, have allowed women to reach the apex of the political pyramid. These are Britain, Ireland, Pakistan, Turkey, Bangladesh, Liberia, India, Germany, Panama, New Zealand and Australia. International organisations have also acknowledged the existence of a gender equality problem and most of them now state in their job adverts that "female applicants are encouraged."

Most societies also discriminate against the disabled, or the physically challenged. In the developing world and even in many developed countries, people born with disabilities or who later become disabled through injury, live difficult lives because the 'system' does not pay much attention to them. In some industrialised countries, special doors and walkways are now added to old public buildings by law, while new buildings are constructed with facilities to address the needs of disabled people. Nowadays, there are international sporting events specifically organised for the disabled, so progress is being made.

From these examples, is it correct to conclude that the wealthier a society becomes, the more attention it pays to the issue of gender equity and the problems of the disabled? Is the problem of 'unjust' discrimination merely a question of economics or do historical and cultural factors have a part to play?

Racism: belief in being superior to others

Let me now move on to the issue of racism that usually arises out of the interrelations between and among people of different skin colours.

First of all, the term *race* defines a group of people of common ancestry. However, race is a complicated concept. One could even argue that there are no distinct races on earth. It is very difficult to make a clear-cut distinction between races! For instance, Professor Kenneth Kidd of Yale University and his team in the United States who have studied the *variability* of the genetic heritage of various ethnic groups have concluded that "in almost any single African population ... there is more genetic variation than in all the rest of the world put together." This means that it can be difficult to classify people into distinct racial groups.

DNA technology may hold clues to the start of human life. A BBC report on September 30, 1998, described research results published by geneticists in the US. After studying twenty-eight population groups in China, academics from the University of Texas and their colleagues in China claimed to have found fresh evidence that Chinese people are descended from Africans. The BBC report stated:

"The findings also add new weight to theories that all human life began in Africa. ... The findings published by the National Academy of Sciences in Washington, supports what has come to be known as the "Out of Africa theory." This theory contends that Homo sapiens, the modern form of human life, is descended from a population of ancestors who migrated out of Africa about 100,000 years ago. The new data also supports the idea of an "African Eve" who is an ancestor of all living humans. The Eve hypothesis, first published in 1987, suggests that all human DNA can be traced back to a single female. This "Eve" would have lived in Africa about 200,000 years ago. The latest research challenges an alternative theory which holds that several different groups of humans evolved separately at the same time in several places around the world. Chinese mythology holds that the Chinese are descended from a single ancestor, the Yellow Emperor. More recent Chinese scholarship has argued that the Chinese evolved separately from other races."

For this discussion, however, I will classify *all* the different races on earth into *five* basic groups as follows: the *Whites*, including 'white' Americans, 'white' Australians, 'white' New Zealanders, 'white' South Africans, all of whom are descended from Europeans, the *Indians* (including native northern and southern Americans); the *Blacks*, including Africans, and any other people of Negro descent elsewhere as well as Aborigines of Australia and Papua New Guinea); the *Arabs* (excluding fair-skinned North Africans); and the *Asians*, including

Chinese, Japanese, and Indians from the sub-continent.

A question one would like to ask is: to which group do children of mixed marriages belong? This is a difficult question. In Germany, children produced from intermarriages between Germans and Africans are almost always characterised as *Black* even if they are as fair-skinned as their German parents. Some people also call children of partly Asian and partly European parentage black. I think that the implication of this classification is that race has shifted from genetics to a socially constructed category on a template that speaks about power relations in society. What do you think?

I will define racism as the belief that certain races of people are by nature superior to others. Members of a racial group holding this belief usually discriminate against members of the other.

Let me make it clear at this juncture that reference to a racial group in this discussion and anything said about the group is not intended to imply that what is said is true for all the members in the group. It is wrong to make sweeping generalisations about any racial group. I note that not all members in a group share the prevailing views that are seen to be characteristic of the group or thought by others to be so. Unfortunately, however, conclusions are always based on the 'dominant' characteristics of an 'important fraction' of the group. Conclusions based on a fraction, even when this is large enough, may not be true about every member of the group. The following discussion is in the context of a simple majority

The belief in one's group being superior to another's is the pillar of racism on which all other extensions are anchored. If you believe that you are superior to others by virtue of your race, then you are a racist. I would class superiority into *moral* and *immoral superiority*. In order to grasp fully the distinction between moral and immoral superiority think about the difference between *believing something* and *feeling something* as you read along.

Moral superiority describes a person's 'feeling' (not 'belief') of superiority about himself or herself. Moral superiority can be associated with personal ambitions, values and principles. A morally superior person 'feels good' about himself or herself with no intention of disrespecting or discriminating against others.

Immoral superiority on the other hand, refers to a person's 'belief' (not 'feeling') that, as a result of his or her ability to transform natural resources into usable materials by means of self-invented machinery, he or she is inherently superior to those who have not been able to do so. Such a person therefore tries to maintain this sense of superiority, by oppressing and repressing others. Public records released in January 1999 in Britain disclosed that the country's most famous World War Two commander, Field Marshal Montgomery, submitted a plan to turn Africa into a white-dominated bulwark against Communism. Lord Montgomery made a secret tour of eleven African countries in 1947 and concluded that Africans were incapable of developing the continent.

There are, of course, cases of immoral superiority which are not fuelled by this ability to transform natural resources into usable materials. They are found within all racial groups, and examples will be presented below. It is important to note that it is immoral superiority that one observes and feels in the world.

I agree that this distinction is somewhat artificial and may appear weak because a feeling held long enough often becomes a belief. However, since the objective of this discussion is to search for a better understanding of the complex concept of racism, let us accept such distinctions as long as they help us achieve our goal.

I discussed the concept of racism and other race issues with at least fifty members in each of the five racial groups I have classified above. Each group comprised young and old people, some as young as six, and others as old as seventy. The objective was not necessarily to make them representative of their racial group, but to get as many people as possible to share their views. In addition, I discussed my definition of racism and other race issues in an Internet discussion forum.

The following responses from the interviews and the Internet discussion are representative of what I received while researching the concept of racism. I shall use letters instead of people's names.

Contributor **A** was of the opinion that my definition of racism omitted something important. He said that racism was not only the belief in being superior, "any form of antagonism directed at another race is racism as well. Such antagonism may be based on reasons other than superiority."

I think that this is an important point. However, the problem is that the antagonistic behaviour referred to is not *always* based on the belief in being superior to the victim. Certainly, such behaviour has been seen in the past – and even today – to be demonstrated mostly by those who believe in their superiority, as in the case of the Nazi and the apartheid regimes and their supporters. However, those that are being discriminated against have also been seen to demonstrate antagonistic behaviour. They do so based on *feelings of anger* at being maltreated because of their colour or something else, and because they resent the people maltreating them for believing or feeling that they are superior human beings. I believe that a behaviour that is based exclusively on such feelings of anger does not deserve to be termed racist. It is a *response* to racism.

If a white or a black individual believes or feels superior to a person in another racial group, he does not need to use violence to maltreat that person. He can simply prevent the supposedly *inferior* person from entering places reserved for himself and members of his group by using such signs as 'WHITES ONLY' or by other more subtle means. He can also deny the supposedly *inferior* person certain rights and privileges which he and his cohorts enjoy. This used to be the case in apartheid South Africa and the southern States of America before the Civil Rights Legislation. It is sometimes also the case in Europe; in fact, instances of this can sometimes be cited all over the world. Clearly, this supposedly *superior* person is not being antagonistic as such. He has simply applied his belief in his superiority. To be able to do this, however, some 'superior' economic, military, linguistic or religious advantage must already exist.

This form of applying a superiority belief can be considered *psychological violence* and is the moral equivalent of an assault. We have seen how this was forcefully resisted in South Africa. The supposedly *inferior* person will fight against such discrimination whenever he can, and sometimes in a violent way. This does not make him a racist. The problem is that as the presumed *inferior* person continues to fight for his rights, the supposedly *superior* person then begins to use force to maintain his advantage. According to one BBC Television report (date and year might be relevant), South Africa's whites, who formed only about five percent of the population, controlled an estimated eighty eight percent of the country's wealth during the apartheid era. In the case of South Africa, antagonistic behaviour from the whites was racist since their *feeling of being superior* had been transformed into a *belief in being superior* which, in their own minds, justified their antagonism towards the Africans.

Some years ago, it was interesting to hear that the National Party (NP) headed by former President de Klerk in South Africa accused the African National Congress (ANC) of racism. *West Africa* (31.10-6.11.94) reports: "De Klerk had told the congress that the ANC had a secret agenda for 'black power' and that 'wild people' were in control of the party."

The ANC retorted that "these NP leaders went so far as to charge President Nelson Mandela with racism ..." In this situation, we note that a former racist oppressor was now calling the formerly oppressed group 'racist'! As Alie Kabba succinctly put it in the same issue of *West Africa*: "the dialogue on race will therefore be marred by the temptation on all sides to believe only in the truth of their specific views." However, the report of South Africa's Truth and Reconciliation Commission revealed that both sides had

committed heinous racist acts; the differences lying in the magnitude of and reasons behind the acts. The ANC has argued that its actions were necessary to fight against widespread racism and the apartheid system.

Please note that I have stated from the outset that a feeling of *moral* superiority is usually personal and private; it is *immoral* superiority that we encounter most commonly in operation in the world. Let us suppose that while feeling morally superior, the individual decides to live amicably with *inferior* people. Would there be any antagonistic reaction from the latter? Perhaps the more appropriate question is this one: Is it possible to feel superior to someone and at the same time treat that person with respect?

As long as the majority of members of a racial group have an *immoral* belief that they are superior to members of other groups, there will be inter-racial tensions. The difficult question, however, is:

on what basis does one conclude that people feel or believe themselves to be superior when both feeling and believing are intangible? The psychological states of 'feeling' and 'believing' are manifest in behaviour as attested in the statement: 'actions speak louder than words!'

The world was surprised in November, 1998, when the public prosecutor in the case against former South African President P.W. Botha said in a BBC interview that there was no concrete evidence that President Botha was responsible for the inhuman acts of his apartheid regime.

Contributor **B** addressed the issue of racial discrimination thus. He looked at racism from a non-violent point of view, arguing that the basic form of discrimination was "the act of distinguishing difference and a showing of partiality and prejudice." She felt that this could also be considered a racist act.

Contributor B's view is much too general for my purpose because that sort of discrimination happens even within racial groups. You cannot call it racism when a black man discriminates against a black man, or a white man against a white man. This is 'class' or 'ethnic' discrimination - other virulent and dangerous forms of bigotry which should not be tolerated. However, that is not what we are discussing now.

Discrimination is only racist when it is based on racial differences and is done by those who consider themselves superior to the other racial group.

Contributor **C** said that "racism is simply a fear of the unknown and both blacks and whites are racists!"

Contributor **D** looked at the whole issue from a different point of view. Instead of starting from the belief in being superior, he suggested that "racism is based on the feeling of inferiority and its complexes." That is, members of a racial group that discriminate against others <u>may</u> be suffering from an inferiority complex.

I reacted to this theory of inherent inferiority complex by asking the following questions: was it an inferiority complex that made South Africa's whites oppress blacks and create "*Whites Only*" areas during the apartheid regime? Were they afraid of the possibility of being asked by their hosts to leave the country? It would be difficult to prove that Apartheid in South Africa did not originate from any other belief among the whites other than that of being superior to the blacks.

Contributor **E** linked racism to the difference in cultures, but I consider his argument evasive and apologetic:

"Racism is a reflection of a very basic cultural difference. At the risk of being simplistic and of thinking stereotypically, blacks, whether in Sierra Leone or here in the US, respond to life in a much more demonstrative way than whites – the rich oral tradition, the extended family, etc., versus the more reserved, stoic culture of European/ American life. So when whites are confronted with the black culture that is vibrant, it is possible that they are alarmed; put off. I'm probably being too general. ..."

Contributor **F** supported my definition of racism by agreeing that the *belief in being superior* should be distinguished from a *feeling of superiority*. He elaborated thus:

"Feeling of superiority is not a genetic endowment but a result of a socialising process. The French 'feel' superior to the English because they are socialised into

22

believing that their culture is more refined and more elegant than that of the British. Could this perception have come from history? The British 'feel' superior to the Americans irrespective of America's wealth. History may play a role here too. ...

Thus humans can feel superior to others for different reasons: a history of dominant or dominated relationship; differences in cultural practices; differences in religion, etc. However, the feeling of superiority in the above situations does not constitute racism because people of the same pigmentation are involved. ...

When the human race is segmented into Black and White, the feeling of superiority assumes a different texture.

It becomes a belief in being superior to the other.

In my view, it is the perception of the Black as subhuman in the history of Black–White relationships that defines racism. Don't ask me about the origin of this! This less human perception of the Black person as reflected in the colour imagery of the

Bible, and in the sociology and politics of genetics reflected in the interpretation of Darwin's Theory, The Bell Curve, etc., has been a major chapter in the curriculum of any White person's informal (in some cases, even formal) education. ...

So, whilst we can all from time to time feel a sense of being more important than the next person, or even intellectually superior to the next person, such a feeling must be distinguished from that in which the other is considered less human, a feeling that could lead to the buying/selling of a person. The French don't consider the English subhuman although the French feel superior. ...

But when the size of one's lips (a genetic factor) is interpreted as a sign of one's intellectual ability, it becomes obvious that racism goes beyond simply feeling superior to a belief."

However, Contributor **G** said:

"Racism surfaces anytime one sets apart a person or people based upon skin colour.

Don't blame the whites and don't blame the blacks. Don't blame any other people: blame greed, hatred, ignorance, etc. and be sure to do it on an individual basis, because everyone is different, no matter the shade of their skins."

A Pecking Order of Racial Superiority

Now, I will discuss the order of racial superiority as I see it practised in the world. My order may not represent what members in the various racial groups believe in or feel about themselves. As I said earlier, discussions on racism are about personal judgements on the feelings and behaviour of others. My pecking order is one of these personal judgements.

Gwyanne Dyer, a London-based historian, recently wrote that "genetic pecking orders are nonsense. Economic pecking orders, on the other hand, are very real." My pecking order is not based on genetics; it is based on social relations as influenced by economics!

My ordering starts from *bottom* to *top*.

I will place blacks at the bottom of my order in terms of the total weight of discrimination they face.

If the assertion that blacks do not demonstrate racial bigotry is true, it should imply that they are the *least* racist. However, this does not imply that there are no black racists. The Truth and Reconciliation Commission in South Africa revealed that some whites endured dreadful acts of racism committed by blacks. There are also examples of racist attacks by blacks on whites in the US. Second from the bottom are the Native American racial group. After the Native Americans come the Arabs. That is, an Arab would consider himself superior to a black man and to a member of the Native American racial group. After the Arabs come the Asians. That is, an Asian would feel superior to a black man, a member in the Native American racial group, and to an Arab.

At the top of the pecking order are the whites, the majority of whom seem to believe that they are superior to members of *all* other races on earth. Whites are, placed at the top of the order because there are, generally, much fewer reported examples of racism against them than there are against members of other racial groups.

My order does not consider differences within racial groups. For instance, I am aware that people in the working class group – irrespective of race – display more racism than those in the middle or upper classes. It is mostly the working class who fear for their jobs and attribute any hardship to the presence of *foreigners* in their communities. This is a cause for antagonistic behaviour. I should qualify that the order of superiority is based primarily on the generality of social relations.

It would be interesting to conduct a study into the relationship between the level of economic development and the superiority complexes of races in the world. Consider my observations below!

The blacks at the bottom of my racial order are seen to be the least in economic power, followed by Native Americans. The oil boom in the Middle East and the Arabs' readiness to invest revenue from oil production in their countries, was creating a more positive image of them in the world before the advent of Islamic terrorism. The economic boom in Asia championed by the Japanese, the South Koreans and the Malaysians, and the potential of the Chinese economy, have improved the Asian image to such an extent that even the whites may now be worried about their first position in the order of superiority. Asians were reported to have donated millions of dollars to a US election campaign, something which was unthinkable before. Also, India and Pakistan have acquired nuclear weapons, demonstrating a high level of technological development. Even isolated North Korea has successfully launched a satellite into space.

In the introduction to his article, 'The Myth of Asia's Miracle' which appeared in the journal *Foreign Affairs* in 1994, Paul Krugman, an American economics professor at Stanford University and recent Nobel Laureate, writes

"Once upon a time, Western opinion leaders found themselves both impressed and frightened by the extraordinary growth rates achieved by a set of Eastern economies. Although these economies were still substantially poorer and smaller than those of the West, the speed with which they had transformed themselves from peasant societies into industrial powerhouses, their continuing ability to achieve growth rates several times higher than the advanced nations, and their increasing ability to challenge or even surpass American and European technology in certain areas seemed to call into question the dominance not only of Western power but of Western ideology."

Now back to my pecking order. Responding to it, Contributor **I** said that "there is no order." According to him, an order would exist only if one believed that it did.

Contributor **J** said that such an order could only have been based on history because "there are many areas in life where the black man is superior to the white man. If white means superior, black means inferior, in which order would you put Michael Jordan and Colin Powell?" he asked. The question is: What about the majority of the blacks in the US? The very few who have achieved remarkable successes form the minority of the minority.

Black and White: Trying to Right the Wrongs?

A number of black leaders in the US fought for the civil rights of blacks living in America. In his "*I have a Dream*" speech, delivered at the 1963 March on Washington, Dr. Luther King Jr. said:

"Five score years ago, a great American, in whose symbolic shadow we stand today, signed the Emancipation Proclamation. This momentous decree came as a great beacon of hope to millions of slaves, who had been seared in the flames of withering injustice. It came as a joyous daybreak to end the long night of their captivity. But one hundred years later, the coloured American is still not free. One hundred years later, the life of the coloured American is still sadly crippled by the manacle of segregation and the chains of discrimination.

One hundred years later, the coloured American lives on a lonely island of poverty in the midst of a vast ocean of material prosperity. One hundred years later, the coloured American is still languishing in the corners of American society and finds himself an exile in his own land. ...

I have a dream that my four little children will one day live in a nation where they will not be judged by the colour of their skin but by their character. ..."

That was indeed a dream, and one that has not yet become a reality even at the beginning of the twenty-first century. After forty-seven years the dream remains largely a dream even though America has recently elected its first black president.

In August 1998, the thirty-fifth anniversary of Martin Luther King's speech US President Bill Clinton called for forgiveness: "It is important that we are able to forgive those we believe have wronged us even as we ask for forgiveness from people we have wronged." John Lewis, the civil rights leader who witnessed King's speech was interviewed on CNN on the thirty-fifth anniversary. He said that "we still have a great distance to go before we can remove all the scars of racism. We're too quiet and too patient."

A year after King's speech, at a meeting on July 5, 1964 shortly after the Civil Rights Act of 1964, Malcolm X – another reputable civil rights leader – had this to say about the white American:

"Prior to one hundred years ago, they didn't need tricks. They had chains. And they needed the chains because you and I hadn't yet been brainwashed thoroughly enough to submit to their brutal acts of violence submissively. ... And it was only after the spirit of the black man was completely broken and his desire to be a man was completely destroyed, then they had to use different tricks. They just took the physical chains from his ankles and put them on his mind."

I have seen and heard about several reports concerning the terrible relationship between black and white Americans. The problems that blacks have faced in the US have been so severe that celebrated black film stars like Sidney Poitier were recruited by white directors and producers to demonstrate this fact in a number of films including "*Guess Who's Coming to Dinner.*" Even though these films were scripted by white writers and financed by white studios, I think that they contributed to creating the awareness of the problems faced by blacks.

In "*Guess Who's Coming to Dinner*", a young white woman from a well-to-do white family falls in love with a distinguished black physician. The young white woman is so much in love with her black doctor that she decides to marry him without the consent of her parents. Her rich father always tells her that all men are equal and that there should not be differences between blacks and whites. But when his daughter brings a black man and introduces him as her future husband, things become difficult. What saves the relationship from collapse is the fact that the black man is a distinguished physician and not just anybody.

Former U.S. President Bill Clinton himself recognised the racial problem and attempted to provide reasons for the divide. In a speech on race relations delivered on October 17, 1995 at the University of Texas, he talked about the facts of racial discrimination in America and appealed to both blacks and whites. I feel that it is important for you to read some of what he said:

"The rift between blacks and whites exists still in a very special way in America. ...

The reasons for this divide are many. Some are rooted in the awful history and stubborn persistence of racism. Some are rooted in the different ways we experience the threats of modern life to personal security, family values and strong communities.

Some are rooted in the fact that we still haven't learned to talk frankly, to listen carefully, and to work together across racial lines. ...

White Americans must understand and acknowledge the roots of black pain. It began with unequal treatment, first in law, and later in fact. African Americans, indeed, have lived too long with a justice system that in too many cases has been and continues to be, less than just. ...

And blacks are right to think something is wrong when the African-American men are many times more likely to be victims of homicide than any other group in this country; when there are more African-American men in our correction system than in our colleges; when almost one in three African-American men in their twenties are either in jail, on parole, or otherwise under the supervision of the criminal system. Nearly one in three. ...

And there is still unacceptable economic disparity between blacks and whites. ...

America, we must clean our house of racism."

And on May 16, 1997, former President Clinton publicly acknowledged an official racist act and apologised on behalf of the US government to Tuskegee survivors of a US government's syphilis experiment that took at least 128 lives. It began in 1932 and lasted for over 40 years until the

Associated Press exposed it in 1972. Three hundred and ninety-nine African-Americans (formerly known as Black-Americans until they came to accept that they are from African ancestry) were told they were getting free medical care, when in fact, they had syphilis, which many did not know, and the government was denying them treatment so researchers could study the disease. This can be classed as an act of *immoral superiority*.

The study took place in Tuskegee, Alabama. By the time it was exposed, 128 men had died, 28 from syphilis and the others from related complications. About 40 wives were infected, and 19 children contracted the disease at birth.

Most Blacks still find life difficult in the US, irrespective of the fact that as slaves, together with the Native Americans, they helped to provide the requisite basis for the country's economic development. Another example of immoral superiority took place in Australia where the Aborigines were only counted as Australian citizens and first allowed to vote in 1967. Can you believe that the Aborigines were governed under flora and fauna laws before 1967? Australia's 300,000 Aborigines are reported to be the most disadvantaged group in Australia's population of 18 million. Their life expectancy is seventeen to twenty years less than that of white Australians. It is reported that many early settlers in Australia even regarded Aborigines as pests and tried to eradicate them from their land by shooting them and poisoning their sources of water.

Theories about race were developed in Europe in order to buttress European superiority, justify 'cleansing' the European race, and colonialism. As more and more scientific evidence is made available that points to the fact that human life originated in Africa, it would be a whole research subject by itself to find out how 'non-Africans' react to the news that they are, after all, Africans by descent.

It was made public in the United States that an early US president, Thomas Jefferson, fathered a child with a slave. CNN wrote on its web site on November 14, 1998 under the title *'Jefferson's West Coast Descendants'*: "DNA evidence virtually proves that one of America's founding fathers had at least one child with a slave." The revelation is generally surprising because President Jefferson was well known for his racism, especially against blacks. Read some of his words: "I advance it therefore as a suspicion only, that the blacks, whether originally a distinct race, or made distinct by time and circumstances, are inferior to the whites in the endowments both of body and mind."

What still haunts German society today is Hitler's action against the Jews, and The Holocaust episode in which millions of Jews were killed in concentration camps. Sadly, however, the several thousands of blacks killed in the concentration camps are hardly ever remembered! Germany has apologised for this action and is trying to do everything possible to right the wrong. The Jews have been fighting for compensation from any country which took a direct or indirect part in the holocaust. The Bank of Switzerland agreed to compensate holocaust victims with more than a billion US dollars for property stolen from them by the Nazis and deposited in Swiss banks. And there was talk about Jewish groups taking German insurance companies to court for their role in The Holocaust. Who will fight for the blacks killed in the concentration camps? I do not think that blacks are expecting the Jews to do this for them. In another section, I will also talk about the call for blacks to be compensated for the slave trade and how this is hardly an issue.

At this point, however, I hasten to mention that the Jews have succeeded in their fight for compensation because they have been united and steadfast in their cause.

The Swedes, the Norwegians, and the Danes on their part once developed racist programmes of "natural selection" on the basis of racial categories even before Hitler's practice became famous. This was made public in 1997.

A very successful 1996 film directed by Hollywood's Steven Spielberg, *Schindler's List,* replays aspects of the terrible holocaust. It however makes one fact clear – that there were good Germans who helped the Jews and protected them from the Nazis.

Blacks in Britain face similar racial discrimination as blacks in the US. After many years of black presence in Britain, it was only following the 1997 elections that the Prime Minister, Tony Blair, made history in naming a black man, Paul Boateng as minister.

A report into the murder of a black youth, Stephen Lawrence, was published in February 1999. The report labels London's police force as being "institutionally racist" and condemns officers for "fundamental errors". The report defines "institutional racism", which is evident in Britain, as "the collective failure of an organisation to provide an appropriate and professional service to people because of their colour, culture or ethnic origin".

The Metropolitan Police at the time, chief Sir Paul Condon admitted the report had brought "shame" to his force. The then Home Secretary said the Race Relations Act would be extended to cover the police.

Blacks also find life difficult in Portugal. The Portuguese were among the first to venture out to Africa when things were difficult in Europe and Africa was rich. They risked their lives in crude sailing boats to look for wealth in Africa. In 1512 King Manuel of Portugal sent an expedition to Congo. The Kingdom of Congo was then a very rich country. In a message to the leader of the expedition, King Manuel wrote: "The expedition has cost us much; it would be unreasonable to send it home with empty hands. Although our principal wish is to serve God and the pleasure of the King of Congo, nonetheless, you will make him understand as though speaking in our name, what he should do to fill the ships, whether with slaves or copper or ivory."

Blacks in France too find it difficult although the French, like the British, colonised several countries in Africa including the Ivory Coast and Guinea. It was recently alleged that the French police killed more than one hundred Algerian immigrants who protested against racial discrimination thirty years ago in France.

In Turkey and in Thailand, Africans are reported to receive inhuman treatment in prisons even when they are merely suspected of crimes. Letters indicating concern about these acts appeared in the August 25-31, 1997 issue of the *West Africa* magazine and in several others.

In Brazil where the majority of the population are people of colour, the minority white population controls the political and economic arenas. In his new book *Violence and Racism in Rio de Janeiro*, retired black Brazilian police office, Colonel Jorge da Silva illustrates the problems of blacks in Brazil.

Blacks face problems everywhere! I decided to ask a friend: "If blacks are having such a terrible time in America and Europe, why don't they go home to Africa where no one will discriminate against them?" He answered:

"My friend, we have to take back from the whites as much as we can. We are all the same people. It is difficult staying here, but we must get compensation in kind. Why not go to Africa and count the numbers of whites and other foreigners out there? Why do you think that the whites did all they can to stay in South Africa and in other parts of southern Africa? Why do you think that the Europeans went to Africa with their colonialism? Why do you think that whenever there is a war or a rebellion somewhere in Africa, we hear that Westerners are being evacuated, but the same Westerners are the first to rush back to the war-torn countries? My brother, it is about survival all over! Whites and other foreigners live in risky mining fields in Africa to earn their living; why should I not live in this risky racist field in the West and earn my living? Okay, okay, the other fact is, most of our leaders in Africa are making things bad for us. Those folks continue to steal the continent's wealth, come overseas and keep the money in banks of already developed countries. Come on, Osman, don't let me cry!"

I let him go because I did not want him to observe the tears in my eyes.

Sports is playing a significant role in trying to reduce racial tensions. Despite the problems which the majority of blacks still face in Europe and America, I commend the exemplary strides taken by countries like France, Holland, England and the US to demonstrate their readiness to embrace their black – or generally foreign professional sports men and women in sports. For instance, these countries send their purely black-skinned citizens to represent them in international competitions.

The many examples I have given above in this section clearly leave the impression that most members of the white race believe or feel they are superior to the blacks. It is, however, erroneous to assume that blacks do not entertain racist feelings or do not demonstrate racist behaviour against whites. I will therefore provide examples to illustrate that the black man can also be racist and has been racist in a number of ways.

Contributor **K**, a woman, came up with this:

"If black men are not capable of feeling superior, let me tell you that some black women are. There are many black women – especially African women – who have the belief that they are superior to men, be they *white*, *black* or *blue*, as long as they are not circumcised men. It does not matter how others look at female circumcision. At least this is the culture that gives me the ability to feel superior! I am being a racist here, call it cultural racism if you will, but I am."

Contributor **L**, another African woman said:

"I agree with the lady who has said that we African women are racists or can be. I live and work in the West and do have contacts with white people, but I shall never date a white man. I just cannot imagine having sexual intercourse with him. I do not have anything against African

47

women who are married to white men or who have white boyfriends or partners. However, I was brought up in Africa to look at African women who have relationships with white men differently. Admittedly, my refusal to date a white man is not logical; it is racist."

Added to what the female contributors have said, I am also aware that in many villages in my country, people find it difficult to accept foreigners as spouses of their daughters or sons, but especially white spouses! There are certainly several reasons other than racist ones for this behaviour, but there is at least a racist one. For example, it was not uncommon at farewell gatherings to hear older Africans tell their children travelling to overseas countries that they should not bring back a spouse whom one could see even with the light off. Can you see why this is racist?

From these few examples, you have been able to see that racism cannot be interpreted from an economic point of view only - economic in the sense that those who discriminate on grounds of colour are usually the more economically advanced in a community. Racism also has a social or cultural bias. The two black women above have used their culture to discriminate against whites.

I will leave this issue for a while and talk about people having a 'community privilege' because of skin-colour. In this regard, let me share with you bits of an article entitled *"White people need to acknowledge benefits of unearned privilege"* which appeared about a decade ago in the *Baltimore Sun* newspaper. It was written by a white professor at the University of Texas in the US who thinks that he has been privileged by the community and that such privilege will continue to exist for whites until "things change." He does not suggest how he expects things to change or when this will happen. He does, however, lament racism and the fact that many whites cannot see it. Interestingly though, he does not say whether racism is good or bad. He says he has benefited because of his colour but it does not make him a bad, unfit or unqualified person and does not even make him a racist. He simply says that in the US, it is the world of the white man. Read some of his words:

"White privilege, like any social phenomenon, is complex. In a white supremacist culture, all white people have privilege, whether or not they are overtly racist themselves. There are general patterns, but such privilege plays out differently depending on context and other aspects of one's identity (in my case, being male gives me other kinds of privilege). Rather than try to tell others how white privilege has played out in their lives, I talk about how it has affected me. ...

I have struggled to resist that racist training and the racism of my culture. I like to think I have changed, even though I routinely trip over the lingering effects of that internalised racism and the institutional racism around me. But no matter how much I 'fix' myself, one thing never changes – I walk through the world with white privilege."

The question for my black readers is: Do blacks experience black privilege in Africa?

I think that the main problem is that whites or Asians living in Africa are also generally those with economic power and can afford a better standard of living than most of the Africans. As a result, they enjoy an 'economic privilege' in Africa and a 'community privilege' in their own countries.

Apparently, most of the examples I have given above have dealt with unfair treatment of people by members of another race. As I indicated earlier, discrimination within the same racial group is also very common.

In this regard, many questions come to mind when we consider the kind of unfair treatment members of the same racial group give to each other.

For example, how can we explain the genocide in Rwanda perpetrated by one ethnic group against another of the same 'black' 'African' race? How do we explain the deep hatred that exists between the Serbs in the former Yugoslavia and their ethnic Albanian counterparts in Kosovo? How do we explain the behaviour of rebel leaders in Sierra Leone whose fighters attack, kill and maim innocent civilians in villages – their own people, who have nothing to do with the politics run in the cities? What about the fight between Catholics and Protestants in Northern Ireland? And the ethnic violence and animosity between Muslims and Christians in Indonesia! North and South Korea! India and Pakistan! Ethiopia and Eritrea! The

Turks and the Kurds! The killing of millions of people in Cambodia by their own people! Why do the Palestinians and the Israelis have such serious problems? Have you considered the reasons for the friction between the Germans – [Europeans] – and East European immigrants – especially the Turks – [Europeans] – living in Germany? Note that it was the Germans who invited these people as 'guest workers' to help rebuild Germany after the Second World War. Do you know why the European Union has not accepted other European countries like Turkey as members?

From the other side, the West African state of Côte d'Ivoire had problems with its immigrant population – millions of Africans from neighbouring countries, who, like the East Europeans in Germany, provided cheap labour and helped build the Ivorian economy after independence from the French. The Côte d'Ivoire had enjoyed peace and economic growth in the sub-region. However, the country suddenly experienced an economic downturn. It was reported that the Ivorian government "is promoting a sense of national identity." An 'African' in Côte d'Ivoire told the BBC that "foreigners – [other Africans] – are treated like dogs by the Ivorians – [Africans]," whilst an Ivorian human rights activist lamented that "this nationalist ideology among Ivorians is at the expense of the harmony that exists between foreigners and Ivorians." Do you understand why this is happening? In the early 1980s Nigeria deported Ghanaian immigrants, accusing them of being one of the reasons why Nigeria was experiencing economic difficulties at the time.

Writing in the newspaper "*For Di People*" of April 14th 1999 in Sierra Leone, Paul Conton described the problem of discrimination in Sierra Leone as follows:

"Perhaps more than any [ethnic group], the Krios have clung to their [ethnic] identity and believed in their cultural superiority. There is a historic undercurrent of discrimination by them against their provincial counterparts, an unwarranted assumption of superiority - cultural, educational and social.

...

Sierra Leone's progress has also been hampered by the rivalry between two much larger ethnic groups, the Mendes and the Themnes, the South/ East and the North. Both groups are continually fighting for political power, each desperate to ensure that the other does not gain an advantage. ...

These two huge divides, the provincial/Krio divide and the Mende/ Themne divide have led directly to our failures."

An aside: I have replaced 'tribe' with 'ethnic group' in Conton's text above since 'tribe' is now used as a negative term and reserved mostly for Africans. One hears Western news reports about 'ethnic conflicts' in Europe but 'tribal conflicts' in Africa. For instance, what makes the Albanians in Eastern Europe an ethnic group but the Themnes in Sierra Leone a tribe? African writers of today should learn to use 'ethnic group' instead of 'tribes' when talking about their people.

The issues raised in the preceding sections are indeed difficult ones. Stop! Give a little bit more thought to them. Can you see a pattern?

You have probably observed that the various types of discrimination result directly from the roles our *history*, our *language*, our *politics*, our *culture*, our *economy*, and our *religion* play in our everyday lives. We use our history to place ourselves somewhere above others; we use politics and our culture to look down on others; we use our economy to determine our values against others; and we use our religion to suppress others who do not share our views. One fact is evident: it is our very selves who are the problem!

The Proposition of Uninfluenced Probability

You certainly would have deduced from the examples I have given in the previous chapter that racial discrimination is a worldwide problem. The examples have also supported my order of racial superiority.

This superiority complex influences people of one race to have very little regard for people of other races. It is therefore necessary to ask one simple but key question: Is there anyone on earth who was able to determine who his or her parents should be?

My friend Dr. James Andrew Weima subscribes to the proposition of uninfluenced probability: *The probability that a child is born to white, black, or any other parents is not influenced by the child.* In other words, a child does not influence the decision about who its parents should be. A white child has to accept its white parents but did not participate in the decision to be born white. The same goes for a black child and for all children born to parents of other races.

One could rightly consider this an everyday reality but certainly children do not usually stop to think that they cannot choose their parents. It makes a lot of difference therefore if parents make this clear whenever they observe that their children demonstrate signs of racial prejudice. Of course this is assuming that the parents themselves do not discriminate against others based on their skin colour.

Why should people believe themselves to be superior to others because they were born to parents of a specific skin colour? Certainly, the answers are many:

1) if one's skin colour enrols him into a 'superior' culture – in technological and industrial terms;

2) if one is able to identify his skin colour with a superior economic birth-right while cultures identifiable with other skin colours are characterised by poverty and disease; and

3) generally, if there is overwhelming evidence of productivity, both material and organisational, and the ability to dominate or impose one's will and enslave others.

I think that if the relative cultural achievements were reversed, blacks would dominate and feel superior to whites. So, is racism really a question of economics?

Clearly, when a child grows up and observes its parents' superior economic status, there is nothing wrong with being proud of its parents' achievement. But if this child grows to believe or feel that it is superior to another based on skin colour, then there is something wrong.

On the question of choosing parents, an African gave an example of how he used to speak to his wealthy parents:

"Every time I made demands on my parents they used to be quite concerned about my propensity for dispensing their money at a rate with which they were not too comfortable, and they inevitably recounted their hard childhood, to which I invariably replied facetiously, 'next time around, choose your parents a bit more carefully. You should have been as smart as I am in choosing you'."

The proposition emphasises the existence of a simple coincidence determined by nature. You are black or white today not because you decided to be black or white. The sooner parents start to teach their offspring about the 'uninfluenced probability,' the better it will be for all, especially for future generations. However, racial groups at the bottom of the order I had proposed must not wait to receive gratuitous equality; they must earn it! They must start with creating order and greater integrity within their groups.

Is it not true that no one is born a racist? Of course, if you consider that the concept of selfishness plays a role in preparing someone for a racist disposition, then you can talk about a biological factor. There is the "selfish gene" in all living organisms which produces the drive to survive and procreate in order to maintain one's species at all cost. That is, all living organisms are born with a trait of selfish attitude which provides the foundation for the development of racist attitudes once influenced by their environments.

Generally, it is the person's immediate environment that influences him/her to become a racist. I therefore subscribe to the proposition of *influenced probability*. By influenced probability I mean that the probability of anyone becoming a racist – believing or feeling that he is superior to another – is influenced by his immediate environment.

The question is, what is Nature's role in people's feeling or belief that they are superior to others? Let me prepare you for the answer to this question. You have seen from the examples so far that racism is largely influenced by economics; those who tend to be branded as racists belong to racial groups that are technologically and industrially developed.

Some believe that Nature has a lot to do with racial differences. The argument goes like this: a thousand year Ice-Age in Africa will create Africans with Nordic instincts of survival and productivity to last them through a snow-bound tomorrow, secure buildings, etc. With a simultaneous steamy hot sun in Europe and America, Europeans and Americans will acquire a tropical mentality and characteristics. The proponents of the Nature theory argue that Africans and Europeans have the same natural equipment, but run on two different software – one is designed by the rigours of the Ice-Age, and the other is programmed by the tropical bounty of easy pickings. They propose that racism is the consequence of the competitive interaction between the products of these two environments.

The Sad Origin of the Complex Problem of Racism

Many scholars of African history reading the heading of this chapter would expect to find a history of events that go way back to the great Ice-Age and even to the Big-Bang theories about the origin of the planets. Others who are less demanding would expect to read about the early European adventurers, sailors, traders, missionaries, slave traders, and colonialists in Africa. Although these are all interesting topics, they are beyond the scope of this book. I will limit this history to the period of The Slave Trade. Certainly, there was a *friendly* encounter immediately preceding The Slave Trade, and one would have liked to investigate the posture of the Africans and their guests, the exchange of pleasantries and gifts, and how the black man presented himself or herself in that transaction that culminated in The Slave Trade. I think that there is extensive literature on these issues and the interested reader is encouraged to try and access some of it. I will cite a few references later on.

With regards to the topic under discussion, as far as the facts of history go, blacks have suffered for a very long time for the development of the white race through the inhuman slave trade. But then, why are blacks not generally seen to be tolerated in white communities? Is it the picture of the slave that others still see when they see a black man? Is it the black colour itself that others do not like? Or have blacks generally done something to deserve such ill- treatment?

In addition to these questions, I have always wished to know whether there is any particular reason, why blacks seem to be generally disadvantaged. I put this question to black, white, and other friends in Germany and in other parts of Europe and America.

Contributor **M** took me back eight centuries:

"From 11th century France, there had been the 'Chanson de Roland'. The hero of the 'Chanson' talks about having to confront 'a cursed race / Black as ink and whose faces / Have nothing white except teeth' – as befits men from 'Ethiopia, a damned land / Of ... big-nosed and flat-eared black people.'

Meanwhile, Saint Jerome (born c. 347, in what is currently Yugoslavia – died c. 420) had been quite typical when he declared that all humans were once 'Ethiopians' – that is black – but had been made so by 'our sins and vices. How? Because sin made us black.' But then when washed, we became 'whiter than snow...' Beyond the symbolic imagery, there is the nitty-gritty thought from Jerome about once seeing his skin 'dirty', in a way that recalled 'the scruffy look of a Negro's epidermis.'

But then, don't forget that crisis in the Book of Numbers between Moses and his Ethiopian wife (chapter 12:1-6), where his brother Aaron and his sister Miriam disapproved. ... There is a long tradition of just not knowing what to do with, how to accommodate, the thought of 'blackness in human form!' Exterminate? Baptise? (as in Acts of the Apostles); Castrate? Enslave? Mock? Celebrate?

All of these, at least eight centuries 'before' the Atlantic version of the same."

Contributor **M**'s talk was insightful. It confirmed my suspicion that this black-white divide did not start from the Trans-Atlantic Slave Trade.

Contributor **N** said that "it is innate to humans to hate another for just being different." In my country Sierra Leone, for example, those who consider themselves 'typical' Sierra Leoneans disliked Fulahs from neighbouring Guinea. Sierra Leoneans merely tolerated the Fulahs. He also expressed the view that the degree of liking was directly correlated to the degree of resemblance. The African is likely to like the black Indian and the Aborigines more than he would like the Arabs, the Asians and the Whites. Similarly, a White man would more likely like the Asians, the Indians, the Arabs better than he would the Aborigines, the Black Indians and the Africans.

Contributor **N** added that the important thing in this dislike/like issue was the reaction of the individual who is disliked. If, for example, the Guinean migrants took to heart the Sierra Leoneans' dislike of them, they would not have become as successful in business as they have been in Sierra Leone. The Fulahs merely ignored the dislike for them, thinking that it would not take the Sierra Leoneans anywhere. The Fulahs were able to contain the discrimination they faced by focusing on their businesses.

Contributor **N** said that he would always advocate the use of the migrant Fulah model for dealing with prejudice in general. Those who travel to other countries and settle there must always try to show understanding for the problems of their hosts and adjust to their realities. He is convinced that if members of discriminated racial groups apply this model by simply ignoring the hostility directed at them and strive to adjust in such circumstances, they could achieve more than when they concentrate their efforts in trying to fight against those who discriminate against them.

Contributor **N**'s suggestion is good, but my fear is that ignoring a problem only perpetuates it. And besides, how much racial discrimination can one ignore? Will the person who discriminates stop doing so if his actions are ignored? I think that the

Fulah example is an isolated case when one considers the examples I have cited so far. A counter example is the case of the Jews who suffered one of the worst consequences of racial discrimination in history. The Jews have not ignored the actions against them; on the contrary, they have achieved success in securing compensation by speaking out.

The question is: What do you think about the relationship between the Jews in Israel and the Palestinians?

Another contributor, **O** - an African - asked me to look at myself for the answer. She said that blacks should not expect outsiders to treat them with respect when their own people did not give them any regard. To support his statement, she elaborated using a chat he once had with a white friend:

"In a friendly manner, a white friend said to me 'You would have been a good slave'.

'I would have fought with you,' I replied jokingly.

He laughed and said 'I would not have attacked you. I would have paid your own brothers to tie you up for me.'

A feeling of guilt and surrender overwhelmed me. I managed to cover up this feeling by accusing my white friend.

'It is because your people created the market,' I said.

We laughed and moved to another topic."

I think that there is something we can learn from this conversation. It is the main stuff on which racist perceptions are built. I will therefore seize this opportunity to delve a bit into slavery and the trade in slaves at this point.

Contributor **O**'s white friend did not take into consideration that Africans too, are human beings. The trade was an economic transaction however cannibalistic it was. White people also sold their own people during the days of slavery in Europe. Today, there are reports about organised groups in East Europe 'selling' children to childless Westerners in the guise of adoption!

Africans are still generally angry about The Slave Trade. They carry vivid pictures in their minds of slaves being shackled with heavy chains on their necks and feet and forced to walk long distances barefoot to sea ports where they were exported to Europe and later to America. Many of them died on their way.

A recent film by Stephen Spielberg depicts a group of Africans bound for slavery in the US. The Africans mutiny and take over the Spanish ship, the 'Amistad'. They try to sail back to Africa but they are captured off the coast of Connecticut. A fierce debate ensues over their fate culminating in a US Supreme Court decision to free them. Even though the film highlights some of the sufferings of the Africans, I feel that its focus is skewed in favour of the American debate on the issue – that the Americans were not the lone 'buyers of Africans' and that even an American President fought for the rights of slaves!

Perhaps the whole problem of the negative black image really started with The Slave Trade. Consequently, today's blacks blame the white man. Unfortunately, although there is an intermittent outcry against The Slave Trade, there does not seem to be a concerted effort by blacks to fight for their cause. But the difficulty could also result from the fact that the entire black race is involved. The Jews are a small group who, according to my racial classification, are Asians even though they are taken today as Europeans. There were blacks who suffered together with Jews in concentration camps. It is the black man himself who should fight for compensation. When a former Nigerian political figure brought up the question of the West compensating black Africa for the inhuman slave trade, I am not sure he was taken seriously by the West.

However, former US president Bill Clinton has said he would consider an apology on behalf of white Americans to African-Americans whose ancestors suffered under the slave trade. People feel that such an apology would be a good gesture if it is accompanied with the right action to improve relations between blacks and whites as well as the conditions of blacks in America.

Contributor **P**, feels that to purge the American society of racism is not an issue of mere 'apologies' and the like. He suggests that:

"There should be a conscious effort to restructure the curricula from kindergarten to tertiary level and beyond (into the professions), that reflect a less poisonous educational content that leads students to question, for example, whether Africans indeed invented anything or have contributed to world civilisation."

Others feel that blacks should recognise and accept an apology from a twentieth century reputable white leader like Bill Clinton who has acknowledged the inhuman role of his forefathers in slavery. It should be clear to all that those who apologise today have no direct responsibility for the acts of their forefathers. They argue that blacks should therefore not continue to vent out their wrath on these innocent people for what happened hundreds of years ago. What 'we' should hold whites responsible for are any wrongs they do us today and not for the wrongs of their ancestors. Similarly, 'we' should be held responsible for our wrongs of today. If a US President is prepared to render an apology, I think that it should be considered as a good step in trying to solidify a positive relation between blacks and whites.

However, what most blacks hardly talk about or fear to talk about is the complicity of Africans in The Slave Trade. I know that such a discussion is unacceptable to many who, because of the enormity of the suffering African slaves went through, are not prepared to look at things from any other perspective. I understand this position because it is the black race that suffered in the inhuman trade. The following response from Contributor **Q,** provides a clear illustration of how the typical black man looks at slavery and the slave trade:

"It was the white man who felt the jobs the Red Indians couldn't do were better done by the black man and so went to Africa and bought himself some blacks."

From this, one would wish to know how the white man came about knowing that the black man was stronger than the Native Americans. History tells us that Europe did not go to Africa to buy slaves. On the contrary, they went there to buy gold and spice. The trade in human beings only started after the Europeans reached the Americas.

It should be noted, however, that even before the white man went to Africa, some form of slavery was already being practised there. History states that there were inter-village/town wars in which African chiefs enslaved captured prisoners of war. The slaves worked for the chiefs on their farms. However, the distinguishing features of this slavery were: 1) the concept of "buying" human beings was non-existent; 2) the form of slavery was quite different to the Trans-Atlantic slave trade as explained by Contributor **R** below; and 3) slavery was not a product of racism; racism was a product of the European slave trade. Contributor **R** explained:

"The African concept of slavery was absolutely different from the West's or the white man's.

Slaves captured in inter-tribal wars were used as servants in royal courts and were not solely used as beasts of burden. Families were not separated. In captivity, a slave was allowed to go along with his wife and children. He was therefore able to maintain his family and culture. Slaves that were used for the purpose of farming were not treated inhumanly. It was possible for them to regain their freedom at some point in the future.

It was based on this notion of slavery and thinking that the white man would accord similar treatment to black slaves that the chiefs engaged in the trade.

Unfortunately, the white man's slavery was race-based, so it was extremely inhuman. The African slaves were seen merely as 'vital components' of the capitalist economic machine which could be used for various functions; the machine could wear out, or could be sold anytime anywhere; African slaves in the West had no provision to regain their freedom. That was why Black Activists like Markus Garvey had to fight for their freedom; they could die and be buried to make the land fertile for future generations, as if they weren't human beings. Are there cemeteries in the US showing where the dead slaves were buried? Where?"

The question is: Is there any justifiable form of slavery?

Slavery, we should remember, has existed in every society known in human history. The Latin word SLAV, from which 'slave' is derived, refers to the present day SLAVIC peoples. They were historically the source of slaves for the European and the Arab world. In 1500, Africans and people of African descent were a minority of the world's slave population. By the year 1700, however, Africans and people of African descent had become the majority. The only explanation for this sudden increase is the European slave trade.

Well, I thought that an in-depth investigation of what really happened before the notorious Trans-Atlantic Slave Trade in which African slaves were taken to US plantations would be useful. I therefore turned again to Contributor **M** who responded as follows:

"By the time of the Trans-Atlantic Slave Trade, the facts and fictions of Africa were in fact already about eight to ten centuries old. It was only in about 1516 - 1517 that the Dominican Friar, Bartholomew de las Casas, proposed that African slaves might be substituted for Amerindians – who were dying 'like fish in a bucket' – both from exploitation and from genetic commingling / disorders. (Las Casas, a passionate defender of Indians, later expressed regrets for this proposal). All the same, there was already a substantive group of African slaves and freed blacks on the Iberian peninsula between 1441-1550."

We learn from history that the white man first visited Africa in search of wealth at a time when things became difficult in Europe. Imagine that the white man risked his life in rickety boats to sail in rough seas just to go and search for wealth in Africa! Some have argued that it was after his arrival that the white man had the opportunity to see African slaves toiling on the farms of affluent black chiefs and rulers. This was how he was able to find out that the Native Americans on his plantations were not as strong as the slaves on the farms of African chiefs. Knowing that the chiefs were eager to acquire arms and ammunition and other Western goods, he persuaded them to *barter* their slaves for his goods. This, they claim, was how the Trans-Atlantic Slave Trade began.

My opinion is that we should condemn the white man for this inhuman trade and not only request an apology but also compensation of some sort. But as we blame the Europeans, we should not underplay the terrible deeds carried out in Africa by Arabs of the Middle East. History has taught us that Arabs kidnapped Africans, mainly in East and Central Africa and took them to the East

African coast. Consequently, if blacks ask for compensation, I would suggest that the leaders think about the following: firstly, companies and governments which compensate the Jews for the Holocaust must be made to compensate descendants of blacks whose forefathers were murdered together with Jews in concentration camps. Secondly, the whites must compensate blacks for the inhuman slave trade. And thirdly, the Arabs must be made to compensate blacks for their inhuman actions against Africans.

What concerns me, however, is the fact that there was some black complicity in the slave trade after the white man created the market for the goods – sadly, the human goods! I am encouraged that a few African writers have addressed this issue. They have done so carefully in order not to trivialise a very important subject. I hope that you will find time to read the following books.

The character Mata Kharibu, a black man in Wole Soyinka's _Dance of the Forests_ (1960) gives this command to his henchmen: "Sell that man down the river! Sell this one down the river!".

In 1968, Ayi Kwei Armah published _The Beautyful Ones Are Not Yet Born._ From it, it is necessary to mention the Voice's statement "He could ask whether anything had changed since the African Chiefs sold their people for the trinkets of Europe."

The writer Ama Ata Aidoo presents a graphic nightmare in her book _Anowa_ (1970) in which the female protagonist dreams a horrific answer to the question of whether "men of the land sold other men of the land" to strangers.

In _Abeng_ (1984), Jamaican Michelle Cliff points at African infighting for providing the conducive environment for the slave trade to the New World. There are also examples in Alejo Carpentier's _The Kingdom of This World_ (1949).

Before you go ....

A lot of people do not discuss race issues because in the end, they are left with more questions than answers. To many, the subject is anathema and it is very difficult for them to read such texts objectively because of their revulsion to the subject.

Where do you stand? If you have come thus far, I believe that you are like me – someone who does not fear to discuss the subject, and someone who thinks it is only when we openly discuss such complex issues that we can find some solutions to the problems that go with them.

As you have seen, this is a subject that cannot be discussed with the requirement that all comments must be based on logic and scientific methods. It is a subject that can also be addressed with emotions even when one tries to maintain objectivity.

I agree that this is an unpleasant topic, but leaving it alone would be doing a disservice to it. I would encourage you, if you will, to reflect on what you have just read – whether the comments were based on logic or not – and to try to contribute in whatever little way to making the world a place for members of all races to live amicably with one another.

I cannot guess how you, as a black or white individual, or as a member in any of the other racial groups will feel after reading this book. If you thought at some point that some of the things I have said were rubbish and you were frustrated along the line, I do understand your frustration. However, if the problem of racism did not exist, I would not be saying things that are likely to disturb you. So, please do what you can in your community to live amicably together with the *foreigner*.

To my dear older Black, Indian, Arab, and Asian readers, one main strategy of controlling racism is to fortify your children by bringing them up to believe in themselves. To my dear older white reader: since most of your children seem all ready to have this strong belief in themselves, your task is to let them understand that they should not feel immorally superior to others.

Admittedly, the racial groups at the lower end of my pecking order have more work to do regarding my call for confidence building in one's self. However, what will continue to remain a threat in all communities is the fact that *bigotry is born out of ignorance.*

I want to thank you for reading. I have enjoyed putting together the views of others and interjecting mine as and when necessary. If, after reading this book, you think that it would be necessary to recommend it to someone, then I will have achieved my objective in writing it.

Other Reflections
by
Osman Alimamy Sankoh (Mallam O.)

By

Professor Sheikh Umarr Kamarah
English Department

SHAW UNIVERSITY

NORTH CAROLINA, USA

Author of *Singing in Exile and The Child of War*
(SLWS, 2002)

Osman Sankoh's *Hybrid Eyes* is not just another in
the catalogue of stories about Africans in Europe, it is a
fresh puff of narrative air, and a compelling story of
tremendous human interest. In this book, the author
focuses on a particularly important "moment" in his
life. The experiences and "encounters" that fill the
space of this "moment" engender a revision of
previously held views, a critical re-evaluation of the

author's own culture, and a bifocal appraisal of the new culture (German) with which the author is confronted.

The book opens with the author waking up to a new physical and cultural environment. We hear him say. "I have been trying to figure out where the hell in the world I am." An African from Sierra Leone, the author is now in Germany in pursuit of higher studies. Osman's story is not new; what is new and of great interest is the way he tells it, and the VISION embodied in the narrative.

The author's narrative style is a blessing to his vision. Because he employs a multiplicity of narrative techniques, Osman is able to "say", dramatise, and interpret his experiences, and at the same time share with his readers, the essence of his message. For example, while following the life of Osman Sankoh, the reader is brought intimately close to the "nature" of racism through the author's use of *DIALOGUE* and *ENGAGEMENT*. In his encounter with the elderly German woman, the author uses dialogue to reveal the thoughts and feelings of the participants with regard to RACE (Colour). But the author goes beyond the dialogue to what I call "engagement," whereby he captures the German lady's attention, exorcises the fear of Blacks in her, and then calmly tells her a story about the origins of Black – skinned and White – skinned people. This method of engagement has an educational value. It allows the breaking of the barriers of ignorance and fear that breed prejudice. The author uses the same technique in his encounter with the little boy in the public transport (S–Bahn). When the little boy refuses to sit near the author and his wife because his mother had told him that "all blacks were niggers," the author engages the little boy. Without rage, but with a sincere intent to "educate" the little boy, the author succeeds to "detoxicate" a young mind. This is a refreshing feature in the story of the African in Europe. It is not about passive complaint; it is about confronting this human issue in a human way.

Osman Sankoh employs the epistolary method to raise and deal with very topical issues. In Andrew's letter from Sierra Leone to the author in Germany, issues of racism, the Western woman, money in Europe (the greener pasture phenomenon), the rebel war in Sierra Leone, and a lot more, are raised. The reader accesses Andrew's views on all of those issues through the author's use of the epistolary method. It is very revealing. The issue expressed in the American proverb, "The grass is always greener on the other side of the fence," is of interest particularly to African readers. Any African, especially one from a large family, who lives in Europe or America, knows about the enormous pressure from relatives and friends to send money back home and to help them come over to the "Greener pasture." It is difficult to convince anyone in Africa that one suffers in many ways in Europe or America. The author uses two lengthy letters that clearly map and discuss the problem. Since people are usually unsatisfied with their lot in life, a modern psychologist has spoken of "The 'Greener Grass' Phenomenon" by which modern individuals continually evaluate supposedly better alternatives for themselves. This basic behavioural truth expressed in a universal metaphor, "The Grass is always Greener on the other side of the fence," the illusion of the land of plenty and luxury, is eloquently dealt with in this book.

Another important issue that the reader is forced to grapple with is that of individual versus group behaviour. In the book, the author's family faces a serious crisis. The author's daughter was born with a hole in the heart and is diagnosed in Sierra Leone while the author and his wife are in Germany. The little girl, Fatima, needs immediate medical attention. The outpouring of sincere human concern and support, both moral and financial, is enormous. Of interest here is the fact that the support comes from both BLACK and WHITE people. The story of Professor Urfer and his wife Barbara, both white Germans, is testimony to the fact that generalisations about human beings are, to say the least, inaccurate. Why then do we have racial tensions around the world? In the words of Carol Tavris, a social psychologist, "Something happens to individuals when they collect in a group. They think and act differently than they would on their own." Osman's book is a perfect laboratory to test the validity of the above theory. This book is certainly one of great human interest.

The narrative of *HYBRID EYES* is laced with humour. Behind the veneer of humour is the author's vision. Differences in cultural practices, and statements about how human perceptions and actions are closely linked with one's world view, are made in a humorous tone. The story of the Sierra Leonean male who brings "flowers" to welcome his loved one is told in a humorous way but speaks volumes about cultural differences. While flowers are important in interpersonal relationships in Europe and America, their function is different in the author's culture. The *BEE* episode is another story told in a humorous way but making a profound statement. Walking in the fields on Professor Urfer and Barbara's farm, Fatmata sees a stray bee and lifts her foot to smash it. Professor Urfer immediately intervenes to save the bee's life saying, "No, it has a right to live." The need for humans to respect the life and dignity of every creature on this planet, and particularly of other humans, is eloquently expressed in Professor Urfer's protest.

The author has injected freshness in the genre of autobiography. While telling his story, he does not merely stand or sit, watch and report, but actively participates in the social drama. He interprets, "engages" other characters, fights back, reflects on issues, evaluates, and tells HIS and OUR story.

The language is intimate, conversational, and accessible. Like the storyteller in Warima, Osman holds a dialogue with the reader. The most interesting aspect of his narrative technique is the intricate interweaving of stories within the story. Since his story in Germany is about encounters, experiences, and slices of other lives, the story switches from one encounter to the other, or from one slice of life to an encounter, without notice. All the little "slices" or "pieces" are intricately tied in one huge examination of – human – nature story. Hybrid Eyes is not only about the experiences of an African in Germany, it is, in a wider context, a reflection on the human condition – black and white. By recognising the beauty and deficiencies in both cultures, by raising prejudice to the level of a universal category, by recognising the role of language in the construction of social reality, by reflecting on the nature of politics in contemporary Africa, and by challenging Mankind to shed the clothing of FEAR and IGNORANCE and embrace one another, *Hybrid Eyes* transcends its physical, temporal, and social setting. *Hybrid Eyes* goes beyond the personal story, and assumes universal appeal. It is the story of everyone everywhere who lives with the "other." It is a story worth reading and discussing in classrooms everywhere.

By

Dr. Lansana Gberie
Canada

Author of *War, Politics and Justice in West Africa*
(SLWS, 2015)

In the many countries in Europe and North America where Africans (and particularly Anglophone Africans) study, Germany is not among the most attractive. There are historical and practical reasons for this, and they have to do with long and concrete associations through colonialism and language. But there is another, altogether less sentimental, reason for the European nation's lack of the easy attractiveness which Britain or France or the United States and Canada afford to the aspiring African scholar or immigrant: it has to do with the aggressively mono-cultural reputation of Germans, a tendency which easily and often violently translates into the kind of racism and racist attacks which has set Germany apart since the Holocaust. For this reason, I approached Osman Sankoh's *Hybrid Eyes*, an account of his experiences as an African student in Germany, with some trepidation, not to say uneasiness. At the end of my first reading, which surprisingly took me only a day, much of my fears were confirmed; but so nuance and subtle is this book that I also emerged with a far deeper appreciation of the various levels of humanism, of the kind of broad-mindedness and kindness of heart among a good number of this much-maligned people which I first came in contact with through my association with Karl Prinz, Germany's former ambassador to Sierra Leone.

The book opens with the author, from the impoverished West African state of Sierra Leone, finding himself in a very wealthy Germany. The wide-eyed observations he makes about his new surroundings are appropriate; the metaphor he uses are crisp and fresh, the language superb. He is in a large room with another Sierra Leonean student named Hudson Jackson. The room's many "rectangular boards of different colours were neatly joined together to form a beautiful pattern." And he compares this room, much too favourably, to his "whitewashed concrete" one at Njala University College in Sierra Leone. Looking through the window, he sees beautifully organised rows and rows of houses reminding him of "pictures I used to see in geography textbooks"; there is a "clean grey street whose long back was covered with a make-up of bright straight white lines and arrows." There is no self-absorption here, and one of the book's appeal is the author's remarkable sense of appreciation for his new surrounding, a foreign country. But it also means that the intensity of feelings and emotions which come with such self-absorption, the kind that helped create great leaders and great autobiographies (Gandhi, Nkrumah), are rather ruefully absent: there is only a man vacillating between appreciation and outrage, not taking a strong position, whining when there is a xenophobic terror, in effect pleading to his hosts for a better understanding and appreciation of Africans and other immigrants; a very normal, intelligent man out to make a good life for himself and others close to him. This is not a world-changing view, but it is no less worthy for it being limited. It is a sound vision, and to show how sound it is, let us look at how another "Third Worlder" recounted his days as a law student in Europe.

In *The Story of my Experiments with the Truth*, Mahatma Gandhi, India's great nationalist leader, recounts his experiences as a young man studying law in Britain. He went to England at the age of 19 in 1888, when he was already married for 6 years. The long journey was by sea, but nowhere in his account does Gandhi describe anything seen or heard that did not relate to him personally. There is no description of the sea or the ship; though Gandhi spent three years in England, no London building is described, no street mentioned, there is no observation about the weather (a favourite pastime in England). But at the time that Gandhi arrived in England, London was the capital of the world, the greatest city on earth, surely something that would not fail to impress a young man from a depressed little town in India. Gandhi's inward concentration was total, his self-absorption fierce. Three years after he arrived in England, Gandhi suddenly becomes a lawyer; the adventure is over: "I passed my examinations, was called to the bar on the 10th of June 1891, and enrolled in the High Court on the 11th. On the 12th I sailed for home." There is what V.S. Naipaul has called a "defect of vision" in Gandhi's whole worldview: the failure to absorb other experiences, to appreciate other cultures, to open up to a changing world. It is the quintessential caste mentality. But this was the foundation of his greatness: the small man in the calico dress, a near-naked man, highly opinionated and bespectacled, bringing down the British Empire.

Osman Sankoh is certainly not Gandhi, and he does not pretend to be so. Still, there are moments of superb engagements with the higher issues in Sankoh's *Hybrid Eyes*. In his interesting review of the book, Sheikh Umarr Kamara has referred to Sankoh's technique of dialogue, which allows for the "breaking of the barriers of ignorance and fear that breed prejudice." There is Sankoh's conversation with the old German lady, which quickly takes the form of Sankoh patiently lecturing the nervous woman on the issue of race, as well as his engagement with the innocent, but already polluted, mind of a German kid who calls him a "nigger" in a subway. These are superb scenes, as much for their sustained humour as for the educational value. They are also revealing of the kind of man Sankoh is: diplomatic, non-confrontational, a patient gentleman, and very, very clever. He is also very brilliant. Germany's graduate programmes, unlike those of North America and the UK, appear to seriously disrespect undergraduate degrees from African universities. So that even though Sankoh had graduated with a distinction in mathematics from the University of Sierra Leone, he is forced to do all his undergraduate courses all over again before he would be allowed into graduate school--some of the courses he had himself taught at Njala. Needless to say, he does it in style, graduating with ones in both his Masters and Ph.D. degrees. In December 1998, he wins the prestigious German Academic Exchange Service (DAAD) prize for "excellent academic performance and extraordinary social engagements by a foreign student", the first African to be so honoured. If his performance does not indicate to the Germans that Africans are not only just as good but could be better, then of course there are more serious issues.

Sankoh is an 'accommodationist'; with him there is always another side to an issue. At the same time that he dreads the brutal and racist German police, the racist pranks of lumpen Germany, he also shows genuine gratitude and affection for those Germans who are truly nice to him and have a totally anti-racist worldview, people like Professor Urfer and his wife Barbara who invites him to their home. Initially a near-sceptic of German humanism, Sankoh's attitude changes dramatically after the painful affair involving his daughter, Fatima. Fatima gets dreadfully ill, with a hole in the heart, in war-ravaged Sierra Leone. A tabloid newspaper campaign in Germany brings in all the help that he needed to fly in Fatima to undergo surgery in Germany.

The list of sponsors included a "female medical doctor" who "put her jewellery on sale with the value of DM 22,000 to help pay" for the surgery. His conclusion: "This is indeed a proof that generalisations about people, be they Europeans, Americans or African, are not good. There are always many people who not fit the generalisations." Just where does this lead one? The reply is nowhere: sit right where you are. Sankoh is not here to inspire you to fight the proletarian or anti-racism war to the finish; his extraordinary brilliance aside, Sankoh is a normal graduate student, an aspiring professional. If he had been Rasa Parks, Sankoh would gently have argued with the white fellows in the bus, patiently lectured them about black humanity and charmed them into not taking him to court for sitting in a "white only" section of the bus (and perhaps there would have been no civil rights movement or Martin Luther King and all those big marches?). When an African explains how he was wrongly accused of stealing, Sankoh laments:

> *Indeed, it is true that some blacks have been*
> *caught in criminal acts. But this is not a*
> *necessary and sufficient reason to put all*
> *blacks in this country into that group. A black*
> *man in Germany is generally perceived to be a poor*
> *man, just like those hungry and starving Africans*
> *shown on German television.*

Hybrid Eyes is no doubt a brilliant narrative, highly readable. There are many memorable passages. Sankoh's descriptions of the many strange things he encounters are often matchless in their eloquence. Here is his encounter with a wooden lift.

> *The lifts here are different. They are small wooden cabins for a maximum of two people at a time that roll continuously up and down. I looked at them suspiciously, went a bit closer, but gave up any attempt to use them. I saw one person come off and another get on. I looked left and right, as if to be sure that no one was watching me to see whether or not I could make it. I moved closer, held tightly to the grip on the wall, raised my foot and waited for the next cabin. I then jumped in quickly.*

The sentences build and add, every word belongs.

The high point of *Hybrid Eyes* is Sankoh's lengthy reply to his brother's letter from Sierra Leone. The two letters deserve to be read very carefully. Young Andrew's letter is enthusiastic, sincerely irresponsible in some places, very acute and sharp in others. The older Sankoh replies in a measured tone, (characteristically) patiently lecturing his brother about how misguided his views are about Germany as the "greener pasture", the drudgery of work he has to ensure to make sure that the deutschmark (always the deutschmark: without the deutschmark Andrew would not write the eloquent letter for he probably wouldn't be at Fourah Bah College: the deutschmark makes all the difference) keep getting to the family in Sierra Leone, the racism he encounters almost on a daily basis, all the worldly troubles. Clearly, Andrew would not be impressed by this argument. In his letter, he kept coming back to the ravages of the war in Sierra Leone, the trouble his family name (although not related to the warlord Foday Sankoh) would cause, the fact that he may not want to sit back all the time expecting to receive the packages from his brother (fruits of the drudgery of work in Germany!). Here, there are really no higher issues discussed; Sankoh knows better than to lecture a sharp and perhaps hungry FBC student about how to change the world.

In *Hybrid Eyes*, we see how incomplete "hybridity" always is, how it is always a process, a precarious and often painful condition, a process of unequal negotiation. Osman Sankoh's book is a treasure for its

96

unabashed and fiercely exact representation of this condition.

By

HASSOUM CEESAY
Gambian Daily Observer
August 10, 1999

This book is long but it is never a boring read. From page one to the end, the reader is inescapably riveted to Osman's ambidextrous weave of countless themes and sub themes about the experiences of an African in Europe - Germany.

The book could thus be called semi-biographical even though the author narrates only a tiny portion of his life - his stay in Germany since the early nineties.

But Osman Sankoh is such a good narrator that he uses flashbacks, letters and telephone messages from home, Sierra Leone, to recount his experiences - both as a youth in the village and as a civil servant in the city - thereby filling the gap to complete his autobiography.

Osman Sankoh arrived in Germany to do a postgraduate course in statistics under a German government scholarship. But that is where the goods ended, at least for a time.

For example, the German college he was to attend would not even allow him to immediately start his course because the authorities weren't sure an African with a degree from an African country will be able to cope with the course. Luckily for the Black race and Osman in particular, he came top of his class and was awarded the top German academic award.

The author also exposes many facets of the life of an African student immigrant in Europe. He discusses the visa curtain, racism both covert and overt, relationships with European women and the participation of African immigrants in development projects back home.

Sankoh has a sharp eye for details. He has meticulously recorded almost all there is to see or experience in the West: the graffitti on walls, "it is seen all over Germany," car theft, the impact of African footballers in the Bundesliga. "Blacks have gained recognition in German sports, a positive step ..." The author ably stresses the impact of such Africans as role models for Black immigrants.

Yet the author uses humour and satire to lampoon the poor performance of Africans in their continent, thus the question "Why Africans always fail at home but succeed in Europe?"

The book also provides an incisive insight into a day in the life of an African immigrant family. The experiences of the author's daughter and his wife in trying to learn the new language and observing decorum like not to throw waste about or to queue for buses, or at the post office.

Such culture shock is adequately depicted by the author to unravel the dichotomy between African and German cultures.

The author's language is concise, crisp and simple. This makes the book well suited for the average reader. His ability to discuss emotive and controversial issues like racism and the adulterous disposition of African couples in the West with humour is exceptional and reveals the makings of a good writer in the author.

This book is recommended for Africans living in Europe or are yearning to travel to Europe. And who is not?

By

HELEN MUENI MAGOLO
The African Courier, Speyer, Germany
June/July, 1999

Western Europe is often perceived by many people in developing countries as a land of hope and opportunity. To many Africans, Western Europe is a place of endless economic opportunities and where poverty and suffering is "non-existent." This perception is sometimes created by Western films and holiday-makers visiting Africa.

Written in direct and simple language, the author, while drawing from his own experiences and observations, discusses the pertinent issues in Germany towards the end of the twentieth century.

Osman arrives in Germany at the time of the fall of the Berlin Wall - the reunification of East and West Germany. His first impressions of Germany is of a highly industrialised country with good infrastructure. However, he soon discovers that, even in this land of wealth and prosperity, poverty does exist. To his surprise, there is an unequal distribution of income, just like in his homeland Sierra Leone, although in no way are the levels of poverty in the two countries comparable. In Sierra Leone and in most of Africa, people continue to face increasing poverty due to unfavourable terms of trade coupled with mismanagement of resources, poor leadership as well as military dictatorships, corruption and political instability which are not suitable environment for economic development.

Contrary to popular belief back home, Germany is not the rosy place it is made out to be. Looking for a house for example, is an African's worst nightmare since some German landlords and landladies are not comfortable renting their houses to foreigners let alone black people. Some Germans would also not entertain the thought of having black neighbours. Even in apartments where Africans live, it may take a long time before Africans can establish any kind of contact with their German neighbours. In public transport and even in the universities, Africans tend to feel isolated in the initial period of their study and without the support of the family, relatives and friends, Germany is indeed a lonely place to live.

As the century comes to a close, Germany is increasingly facing economic difficulties. The once abundant job market is shrinking. Coupled with the opening up of the borders in Europe, there is an increased demand for jobs. Germans are presently competing for the 'black jobs' which were once the reserve of African students and other foreigners as well. In this kind of atmosphere, there is an increasing intolerance by Germans towards Africans and foreigners as a whole.

Most of the difficulties that Africans undergo in Germany, racial discrimination not withstanding, have to do with the stereotypes that Germans have of Africans. As is often portrayed in the Western media, Africa is a continent of poverty, starvation and endless wars. Hence most Africans are perceived as either criminals, illegal immigrants or economic refuges living at the expense of the German tax-payer. The author is also quick to point out that this does not mean that all Africans living in Germany are law-abiding. Africans are also often thought of as being 'foolish' and most Africans have to prove themselves in order to dispel this myth. Even in some German universities, certificates from African universities are looked upon with suspicion and more often than not, African students have to excel in order to gain admission in the courses they intend to study.

The author also points out that not all Germans are racists. The overwhelming support he got from many Germans during his daughter's major surgery, is a case in point. He is therefore of the opinion that both Africans and Germans are people and each should be judged from an individual perspective. He does not rule out the fact though, inspite of there being a minor increase in intermarriages between Germans and Africans, there are still problems of integrating the children of such mixed marriages in society.

In addition, the author also brings out the different cultural perceptions of the two communities. In Africa the role of the family as the backbone of the society is still strong. Both men and women have defined roles which are governed by the traditions and customs of the community.

The author adds that, issues that are not even discussed openly in most of Africa like homosexuality and transsexuality are slowly gaining acceptance in Germany. In the same way, polygamy and female circumcision would be unthinkable among Germans.

He emphasises though, for some of the 'harmful' traditions like female circumcision to be phased out in parts of Africa where it is still practised, the willingness to change must come from within the practising community and from Western pressure.

This book is a good read and it encourages the reader to revisit some of the different perceptions they may hold of the African society and the German society as well.

SIERRA LEONEAN WRITERS SERIES (SLWS)

Focusing on academic, fictional, and scientific writing that will complement other relevant materials used in schools, colleges, universities and other tertiary institutions, the Sierra Leonean Writers Series (SLWS) aims to promote good quality books by Sierra Leoneans and other writers from around the world, writing on themes and issues about Sierra Leone. It is the publisher's hope that students and other readers in Sierra Leone will eventually be at least some of the primary beneficiaries of these works. Not only will people in Sierra Leone be able to read materials that relate to their own lives and experiences, budding writers will also be able to draw inspiration from the efforts of their compatriots and other established writers.

Submitted work undergoes a rigorous peer-review process before being accepted for publication, with an international editorial board providing guidance to writers.

SLWS, based in Warima and Freetown in Sierra Leone, distributes our books globally, including on AMAZON. SLWS co-publishes some titles with Karantha Publishers in Sierra Leone.

For further information, please visit our website: www.sl-writers-series.org
or contact the publisher, Prof. Osman A. Sankoh (Mallam O.) publisher@sl-writers-series.org

Published Books

1	Osman A. Sankoh	2001	*Hybrid Eyes – An African in Europe*
2	Osman A. Sankoh	2001	*Beautiful Colours*
3	Sheikh Umarr Kamarah		*Singing in Exile and The Child of War*
4	Abdul B. Kamara	2003	*Unknown Destination*
5	Samuel Hinton	2003	*The Road to Kenema*
6	Karamoh Kabba	2005	*Morquee – The Political Drama of Wish over Wisdom*
7	Yema Lucilda Hunter	2007	*Redemption Song*
8	Joe A. D. Alie	2007	*Sierra Leone Since Independence – History of a Postcolonial State*
9	Mohamed Combo Kamanda	2007	*The Visa*
10	J Sorie Conteh	2007	*In Search of Sons*
11	Michael Fayia Kallon	2010	*The Ghosts of Ngaingah*
12	J Sorie Conteh	2011	*Family Affairs*
13	Winston Forde	2011	*Layila, Kakatua wan bi Lida*
14	Eustace Palmer Doc P.	2012	*A Pillar of the Community*
15	Siaka Kroma	2012	*Manners Maketh Man – Adventures of a Bo School Boy*
16	Mohamed Combo	2012	*The Price and other Short*

	Kamanda (ed)		*Stories from Sierra Leone*
17	Sigismond Tucker	2013	*From the Land of Diamonds to the Isle of Spice*
18	Bailah Leigh	2013	*Dilemma of Freedom – A Diary from Behind Rebels Lines in the Sierra Leone Civil War*
19	Nnamdi Carew	2013	*Tiger Fist – Two Stories*
20	Yema Lucilda Hunter	2013	*Joy Came in the Morning*
21	Ebenezer 'Solo' Collier	2013	*Primary & Secondary Education in Sierra Leone – Evaluation of more than 50 years of PRACTICES & POLICIES*
22	Gbananom Hallowell	2013	*Gbomgbosoro - Two Stories*
23	Sheikh Umarr Kamarah & Majorie Jones (eds)	2013	*Beg sɔl nɔba kuk sup - An Anthology of Krio Poetry*
24	Siaka Kroma	2014	*Tales from the Fireside*
25	Syl Cheney-Coker*	2014	*The Road to Jamaica*
26	Dr Sama Banya	2015	*Looking Back – My Life and Times*
27	Andrew K Keili,	2015	*Ponder My Thoughts – Vol. 1*
28	Jedidah A. O. Johnson	2015	*Youthful Yearnings*
29	Oumar Farouk	2015	*Landscape of Memories*

			Sesay	
30	Oumar Farouk Sesay	2015	*The Edge of a Cry*
31	Gbanabom Hallowell	2015	*The Road to Kaibara*
32	Mohamed Gibril Sesay*	2015	*This Side of Nothingness*
33	Yema Lucilda Hunter	2015	*Nanna*
34	Yusuf Bangura,	2015	*Development, Democracy & Cohesion*
35	Lansana Gberie,	2015	*War, Politics & Justice in West Africa*
36	Yema Lucilda Hunter	2015	*An African Treasure*
37	Moses Kainwo	2015	*Ayo Ayo Ayo and other Love Songs*
38	Abdulai Walon-Jalloh	2015	*Voices and Passions*

*co-published with Karantha Publishers